Loss Of A Soulmate

Memories of a Grief Journey

Karen E. Passmore

BookLeaf Publishing

India | USA | UK

Made with ❤ on the BookLeaf Publishing Platform
www.bookleafpub.in
www.bookleafpub.com

Dedication

To my Lord and Savior, thank you for eternity.

In loving memory of my husband and soulmate, Jeff. Thank you for our beautiful life together! I will love you forever.

To our daughters, who distracted themselves with friends and games while I secretly wrote this book. ;-)

To my parents, for teaching me how long a blessed marriage can last.

To my sister, for being my best friend since birth and for proofreading. :-D

To my readers, for taking this journey with me.

Preface

Acknowledgements

1. Caring Man

Such a caring man
Husband, dad, friend, and brother --
Loving 'til the end

2. Safe Harbor

You comforted me
When I was stressed or upset --
My safe harbor, gone

3. Too Late

Not simple back pain
But cancer already spread --
Too late to be cured

4. Faith Remains

We prayed for God's will

You passed -- Our hearts are broken

Yet our faith remains

5. Changed

At home with loved ones
You succumbed Thanksgiving week --
We're changed for all time

6. Circle of Gold

A circle of gold

No longer on your finger --

Forever on mine

7. My Peace

Twenty-four blessed years
Together without a fight --
How I miss my peace

8. Sci-Fi

We fancied sci-fi
Star Wars? Star Trek? Both are good
Now I watch alone

9. Gamer

You were a gamer
With family, friends, and all --
As a group, no more

10. Cooking

You enjoyed cooking
Fried rice and "Tom's Mom's Dressing" --
We've not had them since

11. Smile

Your sweet, loving smile
Mischievous smirk on your lips --
So long since we've kissed

12. Touch

I ache for your touch;
Warm arms wrapped tightly 'round me --
Now alone, I'm cold

13. Laughing Green Eyes

Your laughing green eyes
Closed forever to this life --
How I yearn for them

14. Wavy Brown Hair

Your wavy brown hair
I loved its silky softness --
My fingers miss it

15. "Argument"

Our sole "argument:"
Always who loved who "mostest"
Such sweet banter -- lost

16. Sense of Humor

That sense of humor
You could always make me laugh --
Now I grieve and mourn

17. Best Dad

Best dad to our girls
You were loved wholeheartedly --
They both miss you so

18. Cry

When our girls marry,
Who will walk them down the aisle?
We three cry, bereft

19. Memories

Many memories:
Special times spent together --
But now you're not here

20. Soulmate

My best friend... soulmate
God made you "perfect-for-me" --
"'Til death do us part"

21. I Vowed

I'd love you, I vowed,
In sickness, health; until death --
You're gone; I still do...

And I always will.